This meal planner belongs to:

_____

Being on a diet for the year is a wonderful thing to experience. But the truth is this; it is not as easy as it sounds, especially when it comes to meal planning. It was a big pain in the ass whenever I woke up in the morning and remembered that I had to sit down and plan my meals for the day. Of course you have to maintain the macro counts, so you need to do some little calculations. But who on earth has the time to do that every morning of the day?

Definite, not for someone like me. Special diet was not funny until I received the inspiration to draw out a planner to serve me for the whole year. Now I do my diet with style - stress free, budget friendly, and correct macros.

With meal planner you don't need to stress your life every morning of the day, thinking of what to eat and what not to eat. Make out time and plan everything at once, starting from Sunday meals to Saturday meals. Make out time and do your shopping with a well thought out shopping list. The shopping list will also help you to stay on budget.

On each row of the shopping list, you will see a place to list the price of the items you listed for the week. Do you have ideas to add to the planner? Good! There it is – you can now add your meal ideas. This meal planner contains meals ideas for breakfast, lunch and dinner. So, relax and pen down your ideas.

52 weeks of well-planned meals is all you need to stay organized for the whole year without any stress involved. Stick to the planner and see a change in your health.

YOU FIND ANY RECIPE FROM A COOKBOOK? PEN IT DOWN ON THIS PLANNER - THE RECIPE, COOKBOOK TITLE,AND RECIPE PAGE.

BREAKFAST IDEAS

LUNCH IDEAS

DINNER IDEAS

SHOPPING LIST	PRICE	NOTE

SUNDAY	Cal. (kcal)	Net Carb (g)	Fat (g)	Protein (g)	Sugar (g)
BREAKFAST					
LUNCH					
DINNER					
Total Daily Nutrition Fact					

MONDAY	Cal. (kcal)	Net Carb (g)	Fat (g)	Protein (g)	Sugar (g)
BREAKFAST					
LUNCH					
DINNER					
Total Daily Nutrition Fact					

TUESDAY	Cal. (kcal)	Net Carb (g)	Fat (g)	Protein (g)	Sugar (g)
BREAKFAST					
LUNCH					
DINNER					
Total Daily Nutrition Fact					

WEDNESDAY	Cal. (kcal)	Net Carb (g)	Fat (g)	Protein (g)	Sugar (g)
BREAKFAST					
LUNCH					
DINNER					
Total Daily Nutrition Fact					

THURSDAY	Cal. (kcal)	Net Carb (g)	Fat (g)	Protein (g)	Sugar (g)
BREAKFAST					
LUNCH					
DINNER					
Total Daily Nutrition Fact					

FRIDAY	Cal. (kcal)	Net Carb (g)	Fat (g)	Protein (g)	Sugar (g)
BREAKFAST					
LUNCH					
DINNER					
Total Daily Nutrition Fact					

SATURDAY	Cal. (kcal)	Net Carb (g)	Fat (g)	Protein (g)	Sugar (g)
BREAKFAST					
LUNCH					
DINNER					
Total Daily Nutrition Fact					
Total Weekly Nutrition					

WEEK 2

BREAKFAST IDEAS	LUNCH IDEAS

DINNER IDEAS

SHOPPING LIST	PRICE	NOTE

SUNDAY	Cal. (kcal)	Net Carb (g)	Fat (g)	Protein (g)	Sugar (g)
BREAKFAST					
LUNCH					
DINNER					
Total Daily Nutrition Fact					

3

MONDAY		Cal. (kcal)	Net Carb (g)	Fat (g)	Protein (g)	Sugar (g)
BREAKFAST						
LUNCH						
DINNER						
	Total Daily Nutrition Fact					

TUESDAY		Cal. (kcal)	Net Carb (g)	Fat (g)	Protein (g)	Sugar (g)
BREAKFAST						
LUNCH						
DINNER						
	Total Daily Nutrition Fact					

WEDNESDAY		Cal. (kcal)	Net Carb (g)	Fat (g)	Protein (g)	Sugar (g)
BREAKFAST						
LUNCH						
DINNER						
	Total Daily Nutrition Fact					

THURSDAY		Cal. (kcal)	Net Carb (g)	Fat (g)	Protein (g)	Sugar (g)
BREAKFAST						
LUNCH						
DINNER						
	Total Daily Nutrition Fact					

FRIDAY		Cal. (kcal)	Net Carb (g)	Fat (g)	Protein (g)	Sugar (g)
BREAKFAST						
LUNCH						
DINNER						
	Total Daily Nutrition Fact					

SATURDAY		Cal. (kcal)	Net Carb (g)	Fat (g)	Protein (g)	Sugar (g)
BREAKFAST						
LUNCH						
DINNER						
	Total Daily Nutrition Fact					
	Total Weekly Nutrition					

BREAKFAST IDEAS

_____
_____
_____
_____
_____
_____
_____
_____
_____
_____

LUNCH IDEAS

_____
_____
_____
_____
_____
_____
_____
_____
_____
_____
_____

DINNER IDEAS

_____   _____
_____   _____
_____   _____
_____   _____
_____   _____

SHOPPING LIST	PRICE	NOTE

SUNDAY	Cal. (kcal)	Net Carb (g)	Fat (g)	Protein (g)	Sugar (g)
BREAKFAST					
LUNCH					
DINNER					
Total Daily Nutrition Fact					

MONDAY		Cal. (kcal)	Net Carb (g)	Fat (g)	Protein (g)	Sugar (g)
BREAKFAST						
LUNCH						
DINNER						
	Total Daily Nutrition Fact					

TUESDAY		Cal. (kcal)	Net Carb (g)	Fat (g)	Protein (g)	Sugar (g)
BREAKFAST						
LUNCH						
DINNER						
	Total Daily Nutrition Fact					

WEDNESDAY		Cal. (kcal)	Net Carb (g)	Fat (g)	Protein (g)	Sugar (g)
BREAKFAST						
LUNCH						
DINNER						
	Total Daily Nutrition Fact					

THURSDAY		Cal. (kcal)	Net Carb (g)	Fat (g)	Protein (g)	Sugar (g)
BREAKFAST						
LUNCH						
DINNER						
	Total Daily Nutrition Fact					

FRIDAY		Cal. (kcal)	Net Carb (g)	Fat (g)	Protein (g)	Sugar (g)
BREAKFAST						
LUNCH						
DINNER						
	Total Daily Nutrition Fact					

SATURDAY		Cal. (kcal)	Net Carb (g)	Fat (g)	Protein (g)	Sugar (g)
BREAKFAST						
LUNCH						
DINNER						
	Total Daily Nutrition Fact					
	Total Weekly Nutrition					

BREAKFAST IDEAS	LUNCH IDEAS

DINNER IDEAS

SHOPPING LIST	PRICE	NOTE

SUNDAY		Cal. (kcal)	Net Carb (g)	Fat (g)	Protein (g)	Sugar (g)
BREAKFAST						
LUNCH						
DINNER						
	Total Daily Nutrition Fact					

MONDAY		Cal. (kcal)	Net Carb (g)	Fat (g)	Protein (g)	Sugar (g)
BREAKFAST						
LUNCH						
DINNER						
	Total Daily Nutrition Fact					

TUESDAY		Cal. (kcal)	Net Carb (g)	Fat (g)	Protein (g)	Sugar (g)
BREAKFAST						
LUNCH						
DINNER						
	Total Daily Nutrition Fact					

WEDNESDAY		Cal. (kcal)	Net Carb (g)	Fat (g)	Protein (g)	Sugar (g)
BREAKFAST						
LUNCH						
DINNER						
	Total Daily Nutrition Fact					

THURSDAY		Cal. (kcal)	Net Carb (g)	Fat (g)	Protein (g)	Sugar (g)
BREAKFAST						
LUNCH						
DINNER						
	Total Daily Nutrition Fact					

FRIDAY		Cal. (kcal)	Net Carb (g)	Fat (g)	Protein (g)	Sugar (g)
BREAKFAST						
LUNCH						
DINNER						
	Total Daily Nutrition Fact					

SATURDAY		Cal. (kcal)	Net Carb (g)	Fat (g)	Protein (g)	Sugar (g)
BREAKFAST						
LUNCH						
DINNER						
	Total Daily Nutrition Fact					
	Total Weekly Nutrition					

BREAKFAST IDEAS

LUNCH IDEAS

DINNER IDEAS

SHOPPING LIST	PRICE	NOTE

SUNDAY	Cal. (kcal)	Net Carb (g)	Fat (g)	Protein (g)	Sugar (g)
BREAKFAST					
LUNCH					
DINNER					
Total Daily Nutrition Fact					

MONDAY	Cal. (kcal)	Net Carb (g)	Fat (g)	Protein (g)	Sugar (g)
BREAKFAST					
LUNCH					
DINNER					
Total Daily Nutrition Fact					

TUESDAY	Cal. (kcal)	Net Carb (g)	Fat (g)	Protein (g)	Sugar (g)
BREAKFAST					
LUNCH					
DINNER					
Total Daily Nutrition Fact					

WEDNESDAY	Cal. (kcal)	Net Carb (g)	Fat (g)	Protein (g)	Sugar (g)
BREAKFAST					
LUNCH					
DINNER					
Total Daily Nutrition Fact					

THURSDAY	Cal. (kcal)	Net Carb (g)	Fat (g)	Protein (g)	Sugar (g)
BREAKFAST					
LUNCH					
DINNER					
Total Daily Nutrition Fact					

FRIDAY	Cal. (kcal)	Net Carb (g)	Fat (g)	Protein (g)	Sugar (g)
BREAKFAST					
LUNCH					
DINNER					
Total Daily Nutrition Fact					

SATURDAY	Cal. (kcal)	Net Carb (g)	Fat (g)	Protein (g)	Sugar (g)
BREAKFAST					
LUNCH					
DINNER					
Total Daily Nutrition Fact					
Total Weekly Nutrition					

BREAKFAST IDEAS	LUNCH IDEAS

DINNER IDEAS

SHOPPING LIST	PRICE	NOTE

SUNDAY		Cal. (kcal)	Net Carb (g)	Fat (g)	Protein (g)	Sugar (g)
BREAKFAST						
LUNCH						
DINNER						
	Total Daily Nutrition Fact					

MONDAY	Cal. (kcal)	Net Carb (g)	Fat (g)	Protein (g)	Sugar (g)
BREAKFAST					
LUNCH					
DINNER					
Total Daily Nutrition Fact					

TUESDAY	Cal. (kcal)	Net Carb (g)	Fat (g)	Protein (g)	Sugar (g)
BREAKFAST					
LUNCH					
DINNER					
Total Daily Nutrition Fact					

WEDNESDAY	Cal. (kcal)	Net Carb (g)	Fat (g)	Protein (g)	Sugar (g)
BREAKFAST					
LUNCH					
DINNER					
Total Daily Nutrition Fact					

THURSDAY	Cal. (kcal)	Net Carb (g)	Fat (g)	Protein (g)	Sugar (g)
BREAKFAST					
LUNCH					
DINNER					
Total Daily Nutrition Fact					

FRIDAY	Cal. (kcal)	Net Carb (g)	Fat (g)	Protein (g)	Sugar (g)
BREAKFAST					
LUNCH					
DINNER					
Total Daily Nutrition Fact					

SATURDAY	Cal. (kcal)	Net Carb (g)	Fat (g)	Protein (g)	Sugar (g)
BREAKFAST					
LUNCH					
DINNER					
Total Daily Nutrition Fact					
Total Weekly Nutrition					

BREAKFAST IDEAS	LUNCH IDEAS

DINNER IDEAS

SHOPPING LIST	PRICE	NOTE

SUNDAY		Cal. (kcal)	Net Carb (g)	Fat (g)	Protein (g)	Sugar (g)
BREAKFAST						
LUNCH						
DINNER						
	Total Daily Nutrition Fact					

13

MONDAY		Cal. (kcal)	Net Carb (g)	Fat (g)	Protein (g)	Sugar (g)
BREAKFAST						
LUNCH						
DINNER						
	Total Daily Nutrition Fact					

TUESDAY		Cal. (kcal)	Net Carb (g)	Fat (g)	Protein (g)	Sugar (g)
BREAKFAST						
LUNCH						
DINNER						
	Total Daily Nutrition Fact					

WEDNESDAY		Cal. (kcal)	Net Carb (g)	Fat (g)	Protein (g)	Sugar (g)
BREAKFAST						
LUNCH						
DINNER						
	Total Daily Nutrition Fact					

THURSDAY		Cal. (kcal)	Net Carb (g)	Fat (g)	Protein (g)	Sugar (g)
BREAKFAST						
LUNCH						
DINNER						
	Total Daily Nutrition Fact					

FRIDAY		Cal. (kcal)	Net Carb (g)	Fat (g)	Protein (g)	Sugar (g)
BREAKFAST						
LUNCH						
DINNER						
	Total Daily Nutrition Fact					

SATURDAY		Cal. (kcal)	Net Carb (g)	Fat (g)	Protein (g)	Sugar (g)
BREAKFAST						
LUNCH						
DINNER						
	Total Daily Nutrition Fact					
	Total Weekly Nutrition					

14

BREAKFAST IDEAS

LUNCH IDEAS

DINNER IDEAS

SHOPPING LIST	PRICE	NOTE

SUNDAY	Cal. (kcal)	Net Carb (g)	Fat (g)	Protein (g)	Sugar (g)
BREAKFAST					
LUNCH					
DINNER					
Total Daily Nutrition Fact					

15

MONDAY	Cal. (kcal)	Net Carb (g)	Fat (g)	Protein (g)	Sugar (g)
BREAKFAST					
LUNCH					
DINNER					
Total Daily Nutrition Fact					

TUESDAY	Cal. (kcal)	Net Carb (g)	Fat (g)	Protein (g)	Sugar (g)
BREAKFAST					
LUNCH					
DINNER					
Total Daily Nutrition Fact					

WEDNESDAY	Cal. (kcal)	Net Carb (g)	Fat (g)	Protein (g)	Sugar (g)
BREAKFAST					
LUNCH					
DINNER					
Total Daily Nutrition Fact					

THURSDAY	Cal. (kcal)	Net Carb (g)	Fat (g)	Protein (g)	Sugar (g)
BREAKFAST					
LUNCH					
DINNER					
Total Daily Nutrition Fact					

FRIDAY	Cal. (kcal)	Net Carb (g)	Fat (g)	Protein (g)	Sugar (g)
BREAKFAST					
LUNCH					
DINNER					
Total Daily Nutrition Fact					

SATURDAY	Cal. (kcal)	Net Carb (g)	Fat (g)	Protein (g)	Sugar (g)
BREAKFAST					
LUNCH					
DINNER					
Total Daily Nutrition Fact					
Total Weekly Nutrition					

16

WEEK 9

BREAKFAST IDEAS

LUNCH IDEAS

DINNER IDEAS

SHOPPING LIST	PRICE	NOTE

SUNDAY	Cal. (kcal)	Net Carb (g)	Fat (g)	Protein (g)	Sugar (g)
BREAKFAST					
LUNCH					
DINNER					
Total Daily Nutrition Fact					

17

MONDAY	Cal. (kcal)	Net Carb (g)	Fat (g)	Protein (g)	Sugar (g)
BREAKFAST					
LUNCH					
DINNER					
Total Daily Nutrition Fact					

TUESDAY	Cal. (kcal)	Net Carb (g)	Fat (g)	Protein (g)	Sugar (g)
BREAKFAST					
LUNCH					
DINNER					
Total Daily Nutrition Fact					

WEDNESDAY	Cal. (kcal)	Net Carb (g)	Fat (g)	Protein (g)	Sugar (g)
BREAKFAST					
LUNCH					
DINNER					
Total Daily Nutrition Fact					

THURSDAY	Cal. (kcal)	Net Carb (g)	Fat (g)	Protein (g)	Sugar (g)
BREAKFAST					
LUNCH					
DINNER					
Total Daily Nutrition Fact					

FRIDAY	Cal. (kcal)	Net Carb (g)	Fat (g)	Protein (g)	Sugar (g)
BREAKFAST					
LUNCH					
DINNER					
Total Daily Nutrition Fact					

SATURDAY	Cal. (kcal)	Net Carb (g)	Fat (g)	Protein (g)	Sugar (g)
BREAKFAST					
LUNCH					
DINNER					
Total Daily Nutrition Fact					
Total Weekly Nutrition					

BREAKFAST IDEAS

LUNCH IDEAS

DINNER IDEAS

SHOPPING LIST	PRICE	NOTE

SUNDAY	Cal. (kcal)	Net Carb (g)	Fat (g)	Protein (g)	Sugar (g)
BREAKFAST					
LUNCH					
DINNER					
Total Daily Nutrition Fact					

MONDAY	Cal. (kcal)	Net Carb (g)	Fat (g)	Protein (g)	Sugar (g)
BREAKFAST					
LUNCH					
DINNER					
Total Daily Nutrition Fact					

TUESDAY	Cal. (kcal)	Net Carb (g)	Fat (g)	Protein (g)	Sugar (g)
BREAKFAST					
LUNCH					
DINNER					
Total Daily Nutrition Fact					

WEDNESDAY	Cal. (kcal)	Net Carb (g)	Fat (g)	Protein (g)	Sugar (g)
BREAKFAST					
LUNCH					
DINNER					
Total Daily Nutrition Fact					

THURSDAY	Cal. (kcal)	Net Carb (g)	Fat (g)	Protein (g)	Sugar (g)
BREAKFAST					
LUNCH					
DINNER					
Total Daily Nutrition Fact					

FRIDAY	Cal. (kcal)	Net Carb (g)	Fat (g)	Protein (g)	Sugar (g)
BREAKFAST					
LUNCH					
DINNER					
Total Daily Nutrition Fact					

SATURDAY	Cal. (kcal)	Net Carb (g)	Fat (g)	Protein (g)	Sugar (g)
BREAKFAST					
LUNCH					
DINNER					
Total Daily Nutrition Fact					
Total Weekly Nutrition					

BREAKFAST IDEAS

LUNCH IDEAS

DINNER IDEAS

SHOPPING LIST	PRICE	NOTE

SUNDAY	Cal. (kcal)	Net Carb (g)	Fat (g)	Protein (g)	Sugar (g)
BREAKFAST					
LUNCH					
DINNER					
Total Daily Nutrition Fact					

MONDAY		Cal. (kcal)	Net Carb (g)	Fat (g)	Protein (g)	Sugar (g)
BREAKFAST						
LUNCH						
DINNER						
	Total Daily Nutrition Fact					

TUESDAY		Cal. (kcal)	Net Carb (g)	Fat (g)	Protein (g)	Sugar (g)
BREAKFAST						
LUNCH						
DINNER						
	Total Daily Nutrition Fact					

WEDNESDAY		Cal. (kcal)	Net Carb (g)	Fat (g)	Protein (g)	Sugar (g)
BREAKFAST						
LUNCH						
DINNER						
	Total Daily Nutrition Fact					

THURSDAY		Cal. (kcal)	Net Carb (g)	Fat (g)	Protein (g)	Sugar (g)
BREAKFAST						
LUNCH						
DINNER						
	Total Daily Nutrition Fact					

FRIDAY		Cal. (kcal)	Net Carb (g)	Fat (g)	Protein (g)	Sugar (g)
BREAKFAST						
LUNCH						
DINNER						
	Total Daily Nutrition Fact					

SATURDAY		Cal. (kcal)	Net Carb (g)	Fat (g)	Protein (g)	Sugar (g)
BREAKFAST						
LUNCH						
DINNER						
	Total Daily Nutrition Fact					
	Total Weekly Nutrition					

BREAKFAST IDEAS

LUNCH IDEAS

DINNER IDEAS

SHOPPING LIST	PRICE	NOTE

SUNDAY	Cal. (kcal)	Net Carb (g)	Fat (g)	Protein (g)	Sugar (g)
BREAKFAST					
LUNCH					
DINNER					
Total Daily Nutrition Fact					

MONDAY		Cal. (kcal)	Net Carb (g)	Fat (g)	Protein (g)	Sugar (g)
BREAKFAST						
LUNCH						
DINNER						
	Total Daily Nutrition Fact					

TUESDAY		Cal. (kcal)	Net Carb (g)	Fat (g)	Protein (g)	Sugar (g)
BREAKFAST						
LUNCH						
DINNER						
	Total Daily Nutrition Fact					

WEDNESDAY		Cal. (kcal)	Net Carb (g)	Fat (g)	Protein (g)	Sugar (g)
BREAKFAST						
LUNCH						
DINNER						
	Total Daily Nutrition Fact					

THURSDAY		Cal. (kcal)	Net Carb (g)	Fat (g)	Protein (g)	Sugar (g)
BREAKFAST						
LUNCH						
DINNER						
	Total Daily Nutrition Fact					

FRIDAY		Cal. (kcal)	Net Carb (g)	Fat (g)	Protein (g)	Sugar (g)
BREAKFAST						
LUNCH						
DINNER						
	Total Daily Nutrition Fact					

SATURDAY		Cal. (kcal)	Net Carb (g)	Fat (g)	Protein (g)	Sugar (g)
BREAKFAST						
LUNCH						
DINNER						
	Total Daily Nutrition Fact					
	Total Weekly Nutrition					

BREAKFAST IDEAS

LUNCH IDEAS

DINNER IDEAS

SHOPPING LIST	PRICE	NOTE

SUNDAY	Cal. (kcal)	Net Carb (g)	Fat (g)	Protein (g)	Sugar (g)
BREAKFAST					
LUNCH					
DINNER					
Total Daily Nutrition Fact					

MONDAY		Cal. (kcal)	Net Carb (g)	Fat (g)	Protein (g)	Sugar (g)
BREAKFAST						
LUNCH						
DINNER						
	Total Daily Nutrition Fact					

TUESDAY		Cal. (kcal)	Net Carb (g)	Fat (g)	Protein (g)	Sugar (g)
BREAKFAST						
LUNCH						
DINNER						
	Total Daily Nutrition Fact					

WEDNESDAY		Cal. (kcal)	Net Carb (g)	Fat (g)	Protein (g)	Sugar (g)
BREAKFAST						
LUNCH						
DINNER						
	Total Daily Nutrition Fact					

THURSDAY		Cal. (kcal)	Net Carb (g)	Fat (g)	Protein (g)	Sugar (g)
BREAKFAST						
LUNCH						
DINNER						
	Total Daily Nutrition Fact					

FRIDAY		Cal. (kcal)	Net Carb (g)	Fat (g)	Protein (g)	Sugar (g)
BREAKFAST						
LUNCH						
DINNER						
	Total Daily Nutrition Fact					

SATURDAY		Cal. (kcal)	Net Carb (g)	Fat (g)	Protein (g)	Sugar (g)
BREAKFAST						
LUNCH						
DINNER						
	Total Daily Nutrition Fact					
	Total Weekly Nutrition					

BREAKFAST IDEAS

LUNCH IDEAS

DINNER IDEAS

SHOPPING LIST	PRICE	NOTE

SUNDAY	Cal. (kcal)	Net Carb (g)	Fat (g)	Protein (g)	Sugar (g)
BREAKFAST					
LUNCH					
DINNER					
Total Daily Nutrition Fact					

MONDAY	Cal. (kcal)	Net Carb (g)	Fat (g)	Protein (g)	Sugar (g)
BREAKFAST					
LUNCH					
DINNER					
Total Daily Nutrition Fact					

TUESDAY	Cal. (kcal)	Net Carb (g)	Fat (g)	Protein (g)	Sugar (g)
BREAKFAST					
LUNCH					
DINNER					
Total Daily Nutrition Fact					

WEDNESDAY	Cal. (kcal)	Net Carb (g)	Fat (g)	Protein (g)	Sugar (g)
BREAKFAST					
LUNCH					
DINNER					
Total Daily Nutrition Fact					

THURSDAY	Cal. (kcal)	Net Carb (g)	Fat (g)	Protein (g)	Sugar (g)
BREAKFAST					
LUNCH					
DINNER					
Total Daily Nutrition Fact					

FRIDAY	Cal. (kcal)	Net Carb (g)	Fat (g)	Protein (g)	Sugar (g)
BREAKFAST					
LUNCH					
DINNER					
Total Daily Nutrition Fact					

SATURDAY	Cal. (kcal)	Net Carb (g)	Fat (g)	Protein (g)	Sugar (g)
BREAKFAST					
LUNCH					
DINNER					
Total Daily Nutrition Fact					
Total Weekly Nutrition					

BREAKFAST IDEAS	LUNCH IDEAS

DINNER IDEAS

SHOPPING LIST	PRICE	NOTE

SUNDAY		Cal. (kcal)	Net Carb (g)	Fat (g)	Protein (g)	Sugar (g)
BREAKFAST						
LUNCH						
DINNER						
	Total Daily Nutrition Fact					

MONDAY	Cal. (kcal)	Net Carb (g)	Fat (g)	Protein (g)	Sugar (g)
BREAKFAST					
LUNCH					
DINNER					
Total Daily Nutrition Fact					

TUESDAY	Cal. (kcal)	Net Carb (g)	Fat (g)	Protein (g)	Sugar (g)
BREAKFAST					
LUNCH					
DINNER					
Total Daily Nutrition Fact					

WEDNESDAY	Cal. (kcal)	Net Carb (g)	Fat (g)	Protein (g)	Sugar (g)
BREAKFAST					
LUNCH					
DINNER					
Total Daily Nutrition Fact					

THURSDAY	Cal. (kcal)	Net Carb (g)	Fat (g)	Protein (g)	Sugar (g)
BREAKFAST					
LUNCH					
DINNER					
Total Daily Nutrition Fact					

FRIDAY	Cal. (kcal)	Net Carb (g)	Fat (g)	Protein (g)	Sugar (g)
BREAKFAST					
LUNCH					
DINNER					
Total Daily Nutrition Fact					

SATURDAY	Cal. (kcal)	Net Carb (g)	Fat (g)	Protein (g)	Sugar (g)
BREAKFAST					
LUNCH					
DINNER					
Total Daily Nutrition Fact					
Total Weekly Nutrition					

BREAKFAST IDEAS

LUNCH IDEAS

DINNER IDEAS

SHOPPING LIST	PRICE	NOTE

SUNDAY	Cal. (kcal)	Net Carb (g)	Fat (g)	Protein (g)	Sugar (g)
BREAKFAST					
LUNCH					
DINNER					
Total Daily Nutrition Fact					

31

MONDAY	Cal. (kcal)	Net Carb (g)	Fat (g)	Protein (g)	Sugar (g)
BREAKFAST					
LUNCH					
DINNER					
Total Daily Nutrition Fact					

TUESDAY	Cal. (kcal)	Net Carb (g)	Fat (g)	Protein (g)	Sugar (g)
BREAKFAST					
LUNCH					
DINNER					
Total Daily Nutrition Fact					

WEDNESDAY	Cal. (kcal)	Net Carb (g)	Fat (g)	Protein (g)	Sugar (g)
BREAKFAST					
LUNCH					
DINNER					
Total Daily Nutrition Fact					

THURSDAY	Cal. (kcal)	Net Carb (g)	Fat (g)	Protein (g)	Sugar (g)
BREAKFAST					
LUNCH					
DINNER					
Total Daily Nutrition Fact					

FRIDAY	Cal. (kcal)	Net Carb (g)	Fat (g)	Protein (g)	Sugar (g)
BREAKFAST					
LUNCH					
DINNER					
Total Daily Nutrition Fact					

SATURDAY	Cal. (kcal)	Net Carb (g)	Fat (g)	Protein (g)	Sugar (g)
BREAKFAST					
LUNCH					
DINNER					
Total Daily Nutrition Fact					
Total Weekly Nutrition					

BREAKFAST IDEAS

LUNCH IDEAS

DINNER IDEAS

SHOPPING LIST	PRICE	NOTE

SUNDAY		Cal. (kcal)	Net Carb (g)	Fat (g)	Protein (g)	Sugar (g)
BREAKFAST						
LUNCH						
DINNER						
	Total Daily Nutrition Fact					

MONDAY		Cal. (kcal)	Net Carb (g)	Fat (g)	Protein (g)	Sugar (g)
BREAKFAST						
LUNCH						
DINNER						
	Total Daily Nutrition Fact					

TUESDAY		Cal. (kcal)	Net Carb (g)	Fat (g)	Protein (g)	Sugar (g)
BREAKFAST						
LUNCH						
DINNER						
	Total Daily Nutrition Fact					

WEDNESDAY		Cal. (kcal)	Net Carb (g)	Fat (g)	Protein (g)	Sugar (g)
BREAKFAST						
LUNCH						
DINNER						
	Total Daily Nutrition Fact					

THURSDAY		Cal. (kcal)	Net Carb (g)	Fat (g)	Protein (g)	Sugar (g)
BREAKFAST						
LUNCH						
DINNER						
	Total Daily Nutrition Fact					

FRIDAY		Cal. (kcal)	Net Carb (g)	Fat (g)	Protein (g)	Sugar (g)
BREAKFAST						
LUNCH						
DINNER						
	Total Daily Nutrition Fact					

SATURDAY		Cal. (kcal)	Net Carb (g)	Fat (g)	Protein (g)	Sugar (g)
BREAKFAST						
LUNCH						
DINNER						
	Total Daily Nutrition Fact					
	Total Weekly Nutrition					

BREAKFAST IDEAS

LUNCH IDEAS

DINNER IDEAS

SHOPPING LIST	PRICE	NOTE

SUNDAY	Cal. (kcal)	Net Carb (g)	Fat (g)	Protein (g)	Sugar (g)
BREAKFAST					
LUNCH					
DINNER					
Total Daily Nutrition Fact					

35

MONDAY		Cal. (kcal)	Net Carb (g)	Fat (g)	Protein (g)	Sugar (g)
BREAKFAST						
LUNCH						
DINNER						
	Total Daily Nutrition Fact					

TUESDAY		Cal. (kcal)	Net Carb (g)	Fat (g)	Protein (g)	Sugar (g)
BREAKFAST						
LUNCH						
DINNER						
	Total Daily Nutrition Fact					

WEDNESDAY		Cal. (kcal)	Net Carb (g)	Fat (g)	Protein (g)	Sugar (g)
BREAKFAST						
LUNCH						
DINNER						
	Total Daily Nutrition Fact					

THURSDAY		Cal. (kcal)	Net Carb (g)	Fat (g)	Protein (g)	Sugar (g)
BREAKFAST						
LUNCH						
DINNER						
	Total Daily Nutrition Fact					

FRIDAY		Cal. (kcal)	Net Carb (g)	Fat (g)	Protein (g)	Sugar (g)
BREAKFAST						
LUNCH						
DINNER						
	Total Daily Nutrition Fact					

SATURDAY		Cal. (kcal)	Net Carb (g)	Fat (g)	Protein (g)	Sugar (g)
BREAKFAST						
LUNCH						
DINNER						
	Total Daily Nutrition Fact					
	Total Weekly Nutrition					

BREAKFAST IDEAS

LUNCH IDEAS

DINNER IDEAS

SHOPPING LIST	PRICE	NOTE

SUNDAY	Cal. (kcal)	Net Carb (g)	Fat (g)	Protein (g)	Sugar (g)
BREAKFAST					
LUNCH					
DINNER					
Total Daily Nutrition Fact					

MONDAY	Cal. (kcal)	Net Carb (g)	Fat (g)	Protein (g)	Sugar (g)
BREAKFAST					
LUNCH					
DINNER					
Total Daily Nutrition Fact					

TUESDAY	Cal. (kcal)	Net Carb (g)	Fat (g)	Protein (g)	Sugar (g)
BREAKFAST					
LUNCH					
DINNER					
Total Daily Nutrition Fact					

WEDNESDAY	Cal. (kcal)	Net Carb (g)	Fat (g)	Protein (g)	Sugar (g)
BREAKFAST					
LUNCH					
DINNER					
Total Daily Nutrition Fact					

THURSDAY	Cal. (kcal)	Net Carb (g)	Fat (g)	Protein (g)	Sugar (g)
BREAKFAST					
LUNCH					
DINNER					
Total Daily Nutrition Fact					

FRIDAY	Cal. (kcal)	Net Carb (g)	Fat (g)	Protein (g)	Sugar (g)
BREAKFAST					
LUNCH					
DINNER					
Total Daily Nutrition Fact					

SATURDAY	Cal. (kcal)	Net Carb (g)	Fat (g)	Protein (g)	Sugar (g)
BREAKFAST					
LUNCH					
DINNER					
Total Daily Nutrition Fact					
Total Weekly Nutrition					

BREAKFAST IDEAS

LUNCH IDEAS

DINNER IDEAS

SHOPPING LIST	PRICE	NOTE

SUNDAY	Cal. (kcal)	Net Carb (g)	Fat (g)	Protein (g)	Sugar (g)
BREAKFAST					
LUNCH					
DINNER					
Total Daily Nutrition Fact					

MONDAY	Cal. (kcal)	Net Carb (g)	Fat (g)	Protein (g)	Sugar (g)
BREAKFAST					
LUNCH					
DINNER					
Total Daily Nutrition Fact					

TUESDAY	Cal. (kcal)	Net Carb (g)	Fat (g)	Protein (g)	Sugar (g)
BREAKFAST					
LUNCH					
DINNER					
Total Daily Nutrition Fact					

WEDNESDAY	Cal. (kcal)	Net Carb (g)	Fat (g)	Protein (g)	Sugar (g)
BREAKFAST					
LUNCH					
DINNER					
Total Daily Nutrition Fact					

THURSDAY	Cal. (kcal)	Net Carb (g)	Fat (g)	Protein (g)	Sugar (g)
BREAKFAST					
LUNCH					
DINNER					
Total Daily Nutrition Fact					

FRIDAY	Cal. (kcal)	Net Carb (g)	Fat (g)	Protein (g)	Sugar (g)
BREAKFAST					
LUNCH					
DINNER					
Total Daily Nutrition Fact					

SATURDAY	Cal. (kcal)	Net Carb (g)	Fat (g)	Protein (g)	Sugar (g)
BREAKFAST					
LUNCH					
DINNER					
Total Daily Nutrition Fact					
Total Weekly Nutrition					

BREAKFAST IDEAS

LUNCH IDEAS

DINNER IDEAS

SHOPPING LIST	PRICE	NOTE

SUNDAY	Cal. (kcal)	Net Carb (g)	Fat (g)	Protein (g)	Sugar (g)
BREAKFAST					
LUNCH					
DINNER					
Total Daily Nutrition Fact					

MONDAY	Cal. (kcal)	Net Carb (g)	Fat (g)	Protein (g)	Sugar (g)
BREAKFAST					
LUNCH					
DINNER					
Total Daily Nutrition Fact					

TUESDAY	Cal. (kcal)	Net Carb (g)	Fat (g)	Protein (g)	Sugar (g)
BREAKFAST					
LUNCH					
DINNER					
Total Daily Nutrition Fact					

WEDNESDAY	Cal. (kcal)	Net Carb (g)	Fat (g)	Protein (g)	Sugar (g)
BREAKFAST					
LUNCH					
DINNER					
Total Daily Nutrition Fact					

THURSDAY	Cal. (kcal)	Net Carb (g)	Fat (g)	Protein (g)	Sugar (g)
BREAKFAST					
LUNCH					
DINNER					
Total Daily Nutrition Fact					

FRIDAY	Cal. (kcal)	Net Carb (g)	Fat (g)	Protein (g)	Sugar (g)
BREAKFAST					
LUNCH					
DINNER					
Total Daily Nutrition Fact					

SATURDAY	Cal. (kcal)	Net Carb (g)	Fat (g)	Protein (g)	Sugar (g)
BREAKFAST					
LUNCH					
DINNER					
Total Daily Nutrition Fact					
Total Weekly Nutrition					

BREAKFAST IDEAS

_____
_____
_____
_____
_____
_____
_____
_____
_____

LUNCH IDEAS

_____
_____
_____
_____
_____
_____
_____
_____
_____

DINNER IDEAS

_____   _____
_____   _____
_____   _____
_____   _____

SHOPPING LIST	PRICE	NOTE

SUNDAY		Cal. (kcal)	Net Carb (g)	Fat (g)	Protein (g)	Sugar (g)
BREAKFAST						
LUNCH						
DINNER						
	Total Daily Nutrition Fact					

43

MONDAY		Cal. (kcal)	Net Carb (g)	Fat (g)	Protein (g)	Sugar (g)
BREAKFAST						
LUNCH						
DINNER						
	Total Daily Nutrition Fact					

TUESDAY		Cal. (kcal)	Net Carb (g)	Fat (g)	Protein (g)	Sugar (g)
BREAKFAST						
LUNCH						
DINNER						
	Total Daily Nutrition Fact					

WEDNESDAY		Cal. (kcal)	Net Carb (g)	Fat (g)	Protein (g)	Sugar (g)
BREAKFAST						
LUNCH						
DINNER						
	Total Daily Nutrition Fact					

THURSDAY		Cal. (kcal)	Net Carb (g)	Fat (g)	Protein (g)	Sugar (g)
BREAKFAST						
LUNCH						
DINNER						
	Total Daily Nutrition Fact					

FRIDAY		Cal. (kcal)	Net Carb (g)	Fat (g)	Protein (g)	Sugar (g)
BREAKFAST						
LUNCH						
DINNER						
	Total Daily Nutrition Fact					

SATURDAY		Cal. (kcal)	Net Carb (g)	Fat (g)	Protein (g)	Sugar (g)
BREAKFAST						
LUNCH						
DINNER						
	Total Daily Nutrition Fact					
	Total Weekly Nutrition					

BREAKFAST IDEAS

_____
_____
_____
_____
_____
_____
_____
_____
_____

LUNCH IDEAS

_____
_____
_____
_____
_____
_____
_____
_____
_____

DINNER IDEAS

_____   _____
_____   _____
_____   _____
_____   _____

SHOPPING LIST	PRICE	NOTE

SUNDAY	Cal. (kcal)	Net Carb (g)	Fat (g)	Protein (g)	Sugar (g)
BREAKFAST					
LUNCH					
DINNER					
Total Daily Nutrition Fact					

MONDAY		Cal. (kcal)	Net Carb (g)	Fat (g)	Protein (g)	Sugar (g)
BREAKFAST						
LUNCH						
DINNER						
	Total Daily Nutrition Fact					

TUESDAY		Cal. (kcal)	Net Carb (g)	Fat (g)	Protein (g)	Sugar (g)
BREAKFAST						
LUNCH						
DINNER						
	Total Daily Nutrition Fact					

WEDNESDAY		Cal. (kcal)	Net Carb (g)	Fat (g)	Protein (g)	Sugar (g)
BREAKFAST						
LUNCH						
DINNER						
	Total Daily Nutrition Fact					

THURSDAY		Cal. (kcal)	Net Carb (g)	Fat (g)	Protein (g)	Sugar (g)
BREAKFAST						
LUNCH						
DINNER						
	Total Daily Nutrition Fact					

FRIDAY		Cal. (kcal)	Net Carb (g)	Fat (g)	Protein (g)	Sugar (g)
BREAKFAST						
LUNCH						
DINNER						
	Total Daily Nutrition Fact					

SATURDAY		Cal. (kcal)	Net Carb (g)	Fat (g)	Protein (g)	Sugar (g)
BREAKFAST						
LUNCH						
DINNER						
	Total Daily Nutrition Fact					
	Total Weekly Nutrition					

BREAKFAST IDEAS	LUNCH IDEAS

DINNER IDEAS

SHOPPING LIST	PRICE	NOTE

SUNDAY		Cal. (kcal)	Net Carb (g)	Fat (g)	Protein (g)	Sugar (g)
BREAKFAST						
LUNCH						
DINNER						
	Total Daily Nutrition Fact					

MONDAY	Cal. (kcal)	Net Carb (g)	Fat (g)	Protein (g)	Sugar (g)
BREAKFAST					
LUNCH					
DINNER					
Total Daily Nutrition Fact					

TUESDAY	Cal. (kcal)	Net Carb (g)	Fat (g)	Protein (g)	Sugar (g)
BREAKFAST					
LUNCH					
DINNER					
Total Daily Nutrition Fact					

WEDNESDAY	Cal. (kcal)	Net Carb (g)	Fat (g)	Protein (g)	Sugar (g)
BREAKFAST					
LUNCH					
DINNER					
Total Daily Nutrition Fact					

THURSDAY	Cal. (kcal)	Net Carb (g)	Fat (g)	Protein (g)	Sugar (g)
BREAKFAST					
LUNCH					
DINNER					
Total Daily Nutrition Fact					

FRIDAY	Cal. (kcal)	Net Carb (g)	Fat (g)	Protein (g)	Sugar (g)
BREAKFAST					
LUNCH					
DINNER					
Total Daily Nutrition Fact					

SATURDAY	Cal. (kcal)	Net Carb (g)	Fat (g)	Protein (g)	Sugar (g)
BREAKFAST					
LUNCH					
DINNER					
Total Daily Nutrition Fact					
Total Weekly Nutrition					

BREAKFAST IDEAS

LUNCH IDEAS

DINNER IDEAS

SHOPPING LIST	PRICE	NOTE

SUNDAY	Cal. (kcal)	Net Carb (g)	Fat (g)	Protein (g)	Sugar (g)
BREAKFAST					
LUNCH					
DINNER					
Total Daily Nutrition Fact					

49

MONDAY	Cal. (kcal)	Net Carb (g)	Fat (g)	Protein (g)	Sugar (g)
BREAKFAST					
LUNCH					
DINNER					
Total Daily Nutrition Fact					

TUESDAY	Cal. (kcal)	Net Carb (g)	Fat (g)	Protein (g)	Sugar (g)
BREAKFAST					
LUNCH					
DINNER					
Total Daily Nutrition Fact					

WEDNESDAY	Cal. (kcal)	Net Carb (g)	Fat (g)	Protein (g)	Sugar (g)
BREAKFAST					
LUNCH					
DINNER					
Total Daily Nutrition Fact					

THURSDAY	Cal. (kcal)	Net Carb (g)	Fat (g)	Protein (g)	Sugar (g)
BREAKFAST					
LUNCH					
DINNER					
Total Daily Nutrition Fact					

FRIDAY	Cal. (kcal)	Net Carb (g)	Fat (g)	Protein (g)	Sugar (g)
BREAKFAST					
LUNCH					
DINNER					
Total Daily Nutrition Fact					

SATURDAY	Cal. (kcal)	Net Carb (g)	Fat (g)	Protein (g)	Sugar (g)
BREAKFAST					
LUNCH					
DINNER					
Total Daily Nutrition Fact					
Total Weekly Nutrition					

BREAKFAST IDEAS

LUNCH IDEAS

DINNER IDEAS

SHOPPING LIST	PRICE	NOTE

SUNDAY	Cal. (kcal)	Net Carb (g)	Fat (g)	Protein (g)	Sugar (g)
BREAKFAST					
LUNCH					
DINNER					
Total Daily Nutrition Fact					

MONDAY		Cal. (kcal)	Net Carb (g)	Fat (g)	Protein (g)	Sugar (g)
BREAKFAST						
LUNCH						
DINNER						
	Total Daily Nutrition Fact					

TUESDAY		Cal. (kcal)	Net Carb (g)	Fat (g)	Protein (g)	Sugar (g)
BREAKFAST						
LUNCH						
DINNER						
	Total Daily Nutrition Fact					

WEDNESDAY		Cal. (kcal)	Net Carb (g)	Fat (g)	Protein (g)	Sugar (g)
BREAKFAST						
LUNCH						
DINNER						
	Total Daily Nutrition Fact					

THURSDAY		Cal. (kcal)	Net Carb (g)	Fat (g)	Protein (g)	Sugar (g)
BREAKFAST						
LUNCH						
DINNER						
	Total Daily Nutrition Fact					

FRIDAY		Cal. (kcal)	Net Carb (g)	Fat (g)	Protein (g)	Sugar (g)
BREAKFAST						
LUNCH						
DINNER						
	Total Daily Nutrition Fact					

SATURDAY		Cal. (kcal)	Net Carb (g)	Fat (g)	Protein (g)	Sugar (g)
BREAKFAST						
LUNCH						
DINNER						
	Total Daily Nutrition Fact					
	Total Weekly Nutrition					

BREAKFAST IDEAS

LUNCH IDEAS

DINNER IDEAS

SHOPPING LIST	PRICE	NOTE

SUNDAY	Cal. (kcal)	Net Carb (g)	Fat (g)	Protein (g)	Sugar (g)
BREAKFAST					
LUNCH					
DINNER					
Total Daily Nutrition Fact					

MONDAY		Cal. (kcal)	Net Carb (g)	Fat (g)	Protein (g)	Sugar (g)
BREAKFAST						
LUNCH						
DINNER						
	Total Daily Nutrition Fact					

TUESDAY		Cal. (kcal)	Net Carb (g)	Fat (g)	Protein (g)	Sugar (g)
BREAKFAST						
LUNCH						
DINNER						
	Total Daily Nutrition Fact					

WEDNESDAY		Cal. (kcal)	Net Carb (g)	Fat (g)	Protein (g)	Sugar (g)
BREAKFAST						
LUNCH						
DINNER						
	Total Daily Nutrition Fact					

THURSDAY		Cal. (kcal)	Net Carb (g)	Fat (g)	Protein (g)	Sugar (g)
BREAKFAST						
LUNCH						
DINNER						
	Total Daily Nutrition Fact					

FRIDAY		Cal. (kcal)	Net Carb (g)	Fat (g)	Protein (g)	Sugar (g)
BREAKFAST						
LUNCH						
DINNER						
	Total Daily Nutrition Fact					

SATURDAY		Cal. (kcal)	Net Carb (g)	Fat (g)	Protein (g)	Sugar (g)
BREAKFAST						
LUNCH						
DINNER						
	Total Daily Nutrition Fact					
	Total Weekly Nutrition					

BREAKFAST IDEAS

LUNCH IDEAS

DINNER IDEAS

SHOPPING LIST	PRICE	NOTE

SUNDAY	Cal. (kcal)	Net Carb (g)	Fat (g)	Protein (g)	Sugar (g)
BREAKFAST					
LUNCH					
DINNER					
Total Daily Nutrition Fact					

MONDAY	Cal. (kcal)	Net Carb (g)	Fat (g)	Protein (g)	Sugar (g)
BREAKFAST					
LUNCH					
DINNER					
Total Daily Nutrition Fact					

TUESDAY	Cal. (kcal)	Net Carb (g)	Fat (g)	Protein (g)	Sugar (g)
BREAKFAST					
LUNCH					
DINNER					
Total Daily Nutrition Fact					

WEDNESDAY	Cal. (kcal)	Net Carb (g)	Fat (g)	Protein (g)	Sugar (g)
BREAKFAST					
LUNCH					
DINNER					
Total Daily Nutrition Fact					

THURSDAY	Cal. (kcal)	Net Carb (g)	Fat (g)	Protein (g)	Sugar (g)
BREAKFAST					
LUNCH					
DINNER					
Total Daily Nutrition Fact					

FRIDAY	Cal. (kcal)	Net Carb (g)	Fat (g)	Protein (g)	Sugar (g)
BREAKFAST					
LUNCH					
DINNER					
Total Daily Nutrition Fact					

SATURDAY	Cal. (kcal)	Net Carb (g)	Fat (g)	Protein (g)	Sugar (g)
BREAKFAST					
LUNCH					
DINNER					
Total Daily Nutrition Fact					
Total Weekly Nutrition					

BREAKFAST IDEAS

LUNCH IDEAS

DINNER IDEAS

SHOPPING LIST	PRICE	NOTE

SUNDAY	Cal. (kcal)	Net Carb (g)	Fat (g)	Protein (g)	Sugar (g)
BREAKFAST					
LUNCH					
DINNER					
Total Daily Nutrition Fact					

MONDAY	Cal. (kcal)	Net Carb (g)	Fat (g)	Protein (g)	Sugar (g)
BREAKFAST					
LUNCH					
DINNER					
Total Daily Nutrition Fact					

TUESDAY	Cal. (kcal)	Net Carb (g)	Fat (g)	Protein (g)	Sugar (g)
BREAKFAST					
LUNCH					
DINNER					
Total Daily Nutrition Fact					

WEDNESDAY	Cal. (kcal)	Net Carb (g)	Fat (g)	Protein (g)	Sugar (g)
BREAKFAST					
LUNCH					
DINNER					
Total Daily Nutrition Fact					

THURSDAY	Cal. (kcal)	Net Carb (g)	Fat (g)	Protein (g)	Sugar (g)
BREAKFAST					
LUNCH					
DINNER					
Total Daily Nutrition Fact					

FRIDAY	Cal. (kcal)	Net Carb (g)	Fat (g)	Protein (g)	Sugar (g)
BREAKFAST					
LUNCH					
DINNER					
Total Daily Nutrition Fact					

SATURDAY	Cal. (kcal)	Net Carb (g)	Fat (g)	Protein (g)	Sugar (g)
BREAKFAST					
LUNCH					
DINNER					
Total Daily Nutrition Fact					
Total Weekly Nutrition					

WEEK 30

BREAKFAST IDEAS

LUNCH IDEAS

DINNER IDEAS

SHOPPING LIST	PRICE	NOTE

SUNDAY	Cal. (kcal)	Net Carb (g)	Fat (g)	Protein (g)	Sugar (g)
BREAKFAST					
LUNCH					
DINNER					
Total Daily Nutrition Fact					

59

MONDAY	Cal. (kcal)	Net Carb (g)	Fat (g)	Protein (g)	Sugar (g)
BREAKFAST					
LUNCH					
DINNER					
Total Daily Nutrition Fact					

TUESDAY	Cal. (kcal)	Net Carb (g)	Fat (g)	Protein (g)	Sugar (g)
BREAKFAST					
LUNCH					
DINNER					
Total Daily Nutrition Fact					

WEDNESDAY	Cal. (kcal)	Net Carb (g)	Fat (g)	Protein (g)	Sugar (g)
BREAKFAST					
LUNCH					
DINNER					
Total Daily Nutrition Fact					

THURSDAY	Cal. (kcal)	Net Carb (g)	Fat (g)	Protein (g)	Sugar (g)
BREAKFAST					
LUNCH					
DINNER					
Total Daily Nutrition Fact					

FRIDAY	Cal. (kcal)	Net Carb (g)	Fat (g)	Protein (g)	Sugar (g)
BREAKFAST					
LUNCH					
DINNER					
Total Daily Nutrition Fact					

SATURDAY	Cal. (kcal)	Net Carb (g)	Fat (g)	Protein (g)	Sugar (g)
BREAKFAST					
LUNCH					
DINNER					
Total Daily Nutrition Fact					
Total Weekly Nutrition					

BREAKFAST IDEAS

LUNCH IDEAS

DINNER IDEAS

SHOPPING LIST	PRICE	NOTE

SUNDAY	Cal. (kcal)	Net Carb (g)	Fat (g)	Protein (g)	Sugar (g)
BREAKFAST					
LUNCH					
DINNER					
Total Daily Nutrition Fact					

MONDAY	Cal. (kcal)	Net Carb (g)	Fat (g)	Protein (g)	Sugar (g)
BREAKFAST					
LUNCH					
DINNER					
Total Daily Nutrition Fact					

TUESDAY	Cal. (kcal)	Net Carb (g)	Fat (g)	Protein (g)	Sugar (g)
BREAKFAST					
LUNCH					
DINNER					
Total Daily Nutrition Fact					

WEDNESDAY	Cal. (kcal)	Net Carb (g)	Fat (g)	Protein (g)	Sugar (g)
BREAKFAST					
LUNCH					
DINNER					
Total Daily Nutrition Fact					

THURSDAY	Cal. (kcal)	Net Carb (g)	Fat (g)	Protein (g)	Sugar (g)
BREAKFAST					
LUNCH					
DINNER					
Total Daily Nutrition Fact					

FRIDAY	Cal. (kcal)	Net Carb (g)	Fat (g)	Protein (g)	Sugar (g)
BREAKFAST					
LUNCH					
DINNER					
Total Daily Nutrition Fact					

SATURDAY	Cal. (kcal)	Net Carb (g)	Fat (g)	Protein (g)	Sugar (g)
BREAKFAST					
LUNCH					
DINNER					
Total Daily Nutrition Fact					
Total Weekly Nutrition					

WEEK 32

BREAKFAST IDEAS

LUNCH IDEAS

DINNER IDEAS

SHOPPING LIST	PRICE	NOTE

SUNDAY	Cal. (kcal)	Net Carb (g)	Fat (g)	Protein (g)	Sugar (g)
BREAKFAST					
LUNCH					
DINNER					
Total Daily Nutrition Fact					

MONDAY	Cal. (kcal)	Net Carb (g)	Fat (g)	Protein (g)	Sugar (g)
BREAKFAST					
LUNCH					
DINNER					
Total Daily Nutrition Fact					

TUESDAY	Cal. (kcal)	Net Carb (g)	Fat (g)	Protein (g)	Sugar (g)
BREAKFAST					
LUNCH					
DINNER					
Total Daily Nutrition Fact					

WEDNESDAY	Cal. (kcal)	Net Carb (g)	Fat (g)	Protein (g)	Sugar (g)
BREAKFAST					
LUNCH					
DINNER					
Total Daily Nutrition Fact					

THURSDAY	Cal. (kcal)	Net Carb (g)	Fat (g)	Protein (g)	Sugar (g)
BREAKFAST					
LUNCH					
DINNER					
Total Daily Nutrition Fact					

FRIDAY	Cal. (kcal)	Net Carb (g)	Fat (g)	Protein (g)	Sugar (g)
BREAKFAST					
LUNCH					
DINNER					
Total Daily Nutrition Fact					

SATURDAY	Cal. (kcal)	Net Carb (g)	Fat (g)	Protein (g)	Sugar (g)
BREAKFAST					
LUNCH					
DINNER					
Total Daily Nutrition Fact					
Total Weekly Nutrition					

BREAKFAST IDEAS

LUNCH IDEAS

DINNER IDEAS

SHOPPING LIST	PRICE	NOTE

SUNDAY	Cal. (kcal)	Net Carb (g)	Fat (g)	Protein (g)	Sugar (g)
BREAKFAST					
LUNCH					
DINNER					
Total Daily Nutrition Fact					

MONDAY	Cal. (kcal)	Net Carb (g)	Fat (g)	Protein (g)	Sugar (g)
BREAKFAST					
LUNCH					
DINNER					
Total Daily Nutrition Fact					

TUESDAY	Cal. (kcal)	Net Carb (g)	Fat (g)	Protein (g)	Sugar (g)
BREAKFAST					
LUNCH					
DINNER					
Total Daily Nutrition Fact					

WEDNESDAY	Cal. (kcal)	Net Carb (g)	Fat (g)	Protein (g)	Sugar (g)
BREAKFAST					
LUNCH					
DINNER					
Total Daily Nutrition Fact					

THURSDAY	Cal. (kcal)	Net Carb (g)	Fat (g)	Protein (g)	Sugar (g)
BREAKFAST					
LUNCH					
DINNER					
Total Daily Nutrition Fact					

FRIDAY	Cal. (kcal)	Net Carb (g)	Fat (g)	Protein (g)	Sugar (g)
BREAKFAST					
LUNCH					
DINNER					
Total Daily Nutrition Fact					

SATURDAY	Cal. (kcal)	Net Carb (g)	Fat (g)	Protein (g)	Sugar (g)
BREAKFAST					
LUNCH					
DINNER					
Total Daily Nutrition Fact					
Total Weekly Nutrition					

BREAKFAST IDEAS

LUNCH IDEAS

DINNER IDEAS

SHOPPING LIST	PRICE	NOTE

SUNDAY	Cal. (kcal)	Net Carb (g)	Fat (g)	Protein (g)	Sugar (g)
BREAKFAST					
LUNCH					
DINNER					
Total Daily Nutrition Fact					

67

MONDAY	Cal. (kcal)	Net Carb (g)	Fat (g)	Protein (g)	Sugar (g)
BREAKFAST					
LUNCH					
DINNER					
Total Daily Nutrition Fact					

TUESDAY	Cal. (kcal)	Net Carb (g)	Fat (g)	Protein (g)	Sugar (g)
BREAKFAST					
LUNCH					
DINNER					
Total Daily Nutrition Fact					

WEDNESDAY	Cal. (kcal)	Net Carb (g)	Fat (g)	Protein (g)	Sugar (g)
BREAKFAST					
LUNCH					
DINNER					
Total Daily Nutrition Fact					

THURSDAY	Cal. (kcal)	Net Carb (g)	Fat (g)	Protein (g)	Sugar (g)
BREAKFAST					
LUNCH					
DINNER					
Total Daily Nutrition Fact					

FRIDAY	Cal. (kcal)	Net Carb (g)	Fat (g)	Protein (g)	Sugar (g)
BREAKFAST					
LUNCH					
DINNER					
Total Daily Nutrition Fact					

SATURDAY	Cal. (kcal)	Net Carb (g)	Fat (g)	Protein (g)	Sugar (g)
BREAKFAST					
LUNCH					
DINNER					
Total Daily Nutrition Fact					
Total Weekly Nutrition					

BREAKFAST IDEAS

LUNCH IDEAS

DINNER IDEAS

SHOPPING LIST	PRICE	NOTE

SUNDAY	Cal. (kcal)	Net Carb (g)	Fat (g)	Protein (g)	Sugar (g)
BREAKFAST					
LUNCH					
DINNER					
Total Daily Nutrition Fact					

69

MONDAY	Cal. (kcal)	Net Carb (g)	Fat (g)	Protein (g)	Sugar (g)
BREAKFAST					
LUNCH					
DINNER					
Total Daily Nutrition Fact					

TUESDAY	Cal. (kcal)	Net Carb (g)	Fat (g)	Protein (g)	Sugar (g)
BREAKFAST					
LUNCH					
DINNER					
Total Daily Nutrition Fact					

WEDNESDAY	Cal. (kcal)	Net Carb (g)	Fat (g)	Protein (g)	Sugar (g)
BREAKFAST					
LUNCH					
DINNER					
Total Daily Nutrition Fact					

THURSDAY	Cal. (kcal)	Net Carb (g)	Fat (g)	Protein (g)	Sugar (g)
BREAKFAST					
LUNCH					
DINNER					
Total Daily Nutrition Fact					

FRIDAY	Cal. (kcal)	Net Carb (g)	Fat (g)	Protein (g)	Sugar (g)
BREAKFAST					
LUNCH					
DINNER					
Total Daily Nutrition Fact					

SATURDAY	Cal. (kcal)	Net Carb (g)	Fat (g)	Protein (g)	Sugar (g)
BREAKFAST					
LUNCH					
DINNER					
Total Daily Nutrition Fact					
Total Weekly Nutrition					

BREAKFAST IDEAS

LUNCH IDEAS

DINNER IDEAS

SHOPPING LIST	PRICE	NOTE

SUNDAY	Cal. (kcal)	Net Carb (g)	Fat (g)	Protein (g)	Sugar (g)
BREAKFAST					
LUNCH					
DINNER					
Total Daily Nutrition Fact					

MONDAY	Cal. (kcal)	Net Carb (g)	Fat (g)	Protein (g)	Sugar (g)
BREAKFAST					
LUNCH					
DINNER					
Total Daily Nutrition Fact					

TUESDAY	Cal. (kcal)	Net Carb (g)	Fat (g)	Protein (g)	Sugar (g)
BREAKFAST					
LUNCH					
DINNER					
Total Daily Nutrition Fact					

WEDNESDAY	Cal. (kcal)	Net Carb (g)	Fat (g)	Protein (g)	Sugar (g)
BREAKFAST					
LUNCH					
DINNER					
Total Daily Nutrition Fact					

THURSDAY	Cal. (kcal)	Net Carb (g)	Fat (g)	Protein (g)	Sugar (g)
BREAKFAST					
LUNCH					
DINNER					
Total Daily Nutrition Fact					

FRIDAY	Cal. (kcal)	Net Carb (g)	Fat (g)	Protein (g)	Sugar (g)
BREAKFAST					
LUNCH					
DINNER					
Total Daily Nutrition Fact					

SATURDAY	Cal. (kcal)	Net Carb (g)	Fat (g)	Protein (g)	Sugar (g)
BREAKFAST					
LUNCH					
DINNER					
Total Daily Nutrition Fact					
Total Weekly Nutrition					

BREAKFAST IDEAS

LUNCH IDEAS

DINNER IDEAS

SHOPPING LIST	PRICE	NOTE

SUNDAY	Cal. (kcal)	Net Carb (g)	Fat (g)	Protein (g)	Sugar (g)
BREAKFAST					
LUNCH					
DINNER					
Total Daily Nutrition Fact					

MONDAY	Cal. (kcal)	Net Carb (g)	Fat (g)	Protein (g)	Sugar (g)
BREAKFAST					
LUNCH					
DINNER					
Total Daily Nutrition Fact					

TUESDAY	Cal. (kcal)	Net Carb (g)	Fat (g)	Protein (g)	Sugar (g)
BREAKFAST					
LUNCH					
DINNER					
Total Daily Nutrition Fact					

WEDNESDAY	Cal. (kcal)	Net Carb (g)	Fat (g)	Protein (g)	Sugar (g)
BREAKFAST					
LUNCH					
DINNER					
Total Daily Nutrition Fact					

THURSDAY	Cal. (kcal)	Net Carb (g)	Fat (g)	Protein (g)	Sugar (g)
BREAKFAST					
LUNCH					
DINNER					
Total Daily Nutrition Fact					

FRIDAY	Cal. (kcal)	Net Carb (g)	Fat (g)	Protein (g)	Sugar (g)
BREAKFAST					
LUNCH					
DINNER					
Total Daily Nutrition Fact					

SATURDAY	Cal. (kcal)	Net Carb (g)	Fat (g)	Protein (g)	Sugar (g)
BREAKFAST					
LUNCH					
DINNER					
Total Daily Nutrition Fact					
Total Weekly Nutrition					

BREAKFAST IDEAS

LUNCH IDEAS

DINNER IDEAS

SHOPPING LIST	PRICE	NOTE

SUNDAY	Cal. (kcal)	Net Carb (g)	Fat (g)	Protein (g)	Sugar (g)
BREAKFAST					
LUNCH					
DINNER					
Total Daily Nutrition Fact					

75

MONDAY	Cal. (kcal)	Net Carb (g)	Fat (g)	Protein (g)	Sugar (g)
BREAKFAST					
LUNCH					
DINNER					
Total Daily Nutrition Fact					

TUESDAY	Cal. (kcal)	Net Carb (g)	Fat (g)	Protein (g)	Sugar (g)
BREAKFAST					
LUNCH					
DINNER					
Total Daily Nutrition Fact					

WEDNESDAY	Cal. (kcal)	Net Carb (g)	Fat (g)	Protein (g)	Sugar (g)
BREAKFAST					
LUNCH					
DINNER					
Total Daily Nutrition Fact					

THURSDAY	Cal. (kcal)	Net Carb (g)	Fat (g)	Protein (g)	Sugar (g)
BREAKFAST					
LUNCH					
DINNER					
Total Daily Nutrition Fact					

FRIDAY	Cal. (kcal)	Net Carb (g)	Fat (g)	Protein (g)	Sugar (g)
BREAKFAST					
LUNCH					
DINNER					
Total Daily Nutrition Fact					

SATURDAY	Cal. (kcal)	Net Carb (g)	Fat (g)	Protein (g)	Sugar (g)
BREAKFAST					
LUNCH					
DINNER					
Total Daily Nutrition Fact					
Total Weekly Nutrition					

BREAKFAST IDEAS

LUNCH IDEAS

DINNER IDEAS

SHOPPING LIST	PRICE	NOTE

SUNDAY	Cal. (kcal)	Net Carb (g)	Fat (g)	Protein (g)	Sugar (g)
BREAKFAST					
LUNCH					
DINNER					
Total Daily Nutrition Fact					

77

MONDAY	Cal. (kcal)	Net Carb (g)	Fat (g)	Protein (g)	Sugar (g)
BREAKFAST					
LUNCH					
DINNER					
Total Daily Nutrition Fact					

TUESDAY	Cal. (kcal)	Net Carb (g)	Fat (g)	Protein (g)	Sugar (g)
BREAKFAST					
LUNCH					
DINNER					
Total Daily Nutrition Fact					

WEDNESDAY	Cal. (kcal)	Net Carb (g)	Fat (g)	Protein (g)	Sugar (g)
BREAKFAST					
LUNCH					
DINNER					
Total Daily Nutrition Fact					

THURSDAY	Cal. (kcal)	Net Carb (g)	Fat (g)	Protein (g)	Sugar (g)
BREAKFAST					
LUNCH					
DINNER					
Total Daily Nutrition Fact					

FRIDAY	Cal. (kcal)	Net Carb (g)	Fat (g)	Protein (g)	Sugar (g)
BREAKFAST					
LUNCH					
DINNER					
Total Daily Nutrition Fact					

SATURDAY	Cal. (kcal)	Net Carb (g)	Fat (g)	Protein (g)	Sugar (g)
BREAKFAST					
LUNCH					
DINNER					
Total Daily Nutrition Fact					
Total Weekly Nutrition					

BREAKFAST IDEAS

LUNCH IDEAS

DINNER IDEAS

SHOPPING LIST	PRICE	NOTE

SUNDAY	Cal. (kcal)	Net Carb (g)	Fat (g)	Protein (g)	Sugar (g)
BREAKFAST					
LUNCH					
DINNER					
Total Daily Nutrition Fact					

MONDAY	Cal. (kcal)	Net Carb (g)	Fat (g)	Protein (g)	Sugar (g)
BREAKFAST					
LUNCH					
DINNER					
Total Daily Nutrition Fact					

TUESDAY	Cal. (kcal)	Net Carb (g)	Fat (g)	Protein (g)	Sugar (g)
BREAKFAST					
LUNCH					
DINNER					
Total Daily Nutrition Fact					

WEDNESDAY	Cal. (kcal)	Net Carb (g)	Fat (g)	Protein (g)	Sugar (g)
BREAKFAST					
LUNCH					
DINNER					
Total Daily Nutrition Fact					

THURSDAY	Cal. (kcal)	Net Carb (g)	Fat (g)	Protein (g)	Sugar (g)
BREAKFAST					
LUNCH					
DINNER					
Total Daily Nutrition Fact					

FRIDAY	Cal. (kcal)	Net Carb (g)	Fat (g)	Protein (g)	Sugar (g)
BREAKFAST					
LUNCH					
DINNER					
Total Daily Nutrition Fact					

SATURDAY	Cal. (kcal)	Net Carb (g)	Fat (g)	Protein (g)	Sugar (g)
BREAKFAST					
LUNCH					
DINNER					
Total Daily Nutrition Fact					
Total Weekly Nutrition					

BREAKFAST IDEAS

LUNCH IDEAS

DINNER IDEAS

SHOPPING LIST	PRICE	NOTE

SUNDAY	Cal. (kcal)	Net Carb (g)	Fat (g)	Protein (g)	Sugar (g)
BREAKFAST					
LUNCH					
DINNER					
Total Daily Nutrition Fact					

MONDAY	Cal. (kcal)	Net Carb (g)	Fat (g)	Protein (g)	Sugar (g)
BREAKFAST					
LUNCH					
DINNER					
Total Daily Nutrition Fact					

TUESDAY	Cal. (kcal)	Net Carb (g)	Fat (g)	Protein (g)	Sugar (g)
BREAKFAST					
LUNCH					
DINNER					
Total Daily Nutrition Fact					

WEDNESDAY	Cal. (kcal)	Net Carb (g)	Fat (g)	Protein (g)	Sugar (g)
BREAKFAST					
LUNCH					
DINNER					
Total Daily Nutrition Fact					

THURSDAY	Cal. (kcal)	Net Carb (g)	Fat (g)	Protein (g)	Sugar (g)
BREAKFAST					
LUNCH					
DINNER					
Total Daily Nutrition Fact					

FRIDAY	Cal. (kcal)	Net Carb (g)	Fat (g)	Protein (g)	Sugar (g)
BREAKFAST					
LUNCH					
DINNER					
Total Daily Nutrition Fact					

SATURDAY	Cal. (kcal)	Net Carb (g)	Fat (g)	Protein (g)	Sugar (g)
BREAKFAST					
LUNCH					
DINNER					
Total Daily Nutrition Fact					
Total Weekly Nutrition					

BREAKFAST IDEAS	LUNCH IDEAS

DINNER IDEAS

SHOPPING LIST	PRICE	NOTE

SUNDAY	Cal. (kcal)	Net Carb (g)	Fat (g)	Protein (g)	Sugar (g)
BREAKFAST					
LUNCH					
DINNER					
Total Daily Nutrition Fact					

MONDAY	Cal. (kcal)	Net Carb (g)	Fat (g)	Protein (g)	Sugar (g)
BREAKFAST					
LUNCH					
DINNER					
Total Daily Nutrition Fact					

TUESDAY	Cal. (kcal)	Net Carb (g)	Fat (g)	Protein (g)	Sugar (g)
BREAKFAST					
LUNCH					
DINNER					
Total Daily Nutrition Fact					

WEDNESDAY	Cal. (kcal)	Net Carb (g)	Fat (g)	Protein (g)	Sugar (g)
BREAKFAST					
LUNCH					
DINNER					
Total Daily Nutrition Fact					

THURSDAY	Cal. (kcal)	Net Carb (g)	Fat (g)	Protein (g)	Sugar (g)
BREAKFAST					
LUNCH					
DINNER					
Total Daily Nutrition Fact					

FRIDAY	Cal. (kcal)	Net Carb (g)	Fat (g)	Protein (g)	Sugar (g)
BREAKFAST					
LUNCH					
DINNER					
Total Daily Nutrition Fact					

SATURDAY	Cal. (kcal)	Net Carb (g)	Fat (g)	Protein (g)	Sugar (g)
BREAKFAST					
LUNCH					
DINNER					
Total Daily Nutrition Fact					
Total Weekly Nutrition					

BREAKFAST IDEAS

LUNCH IDEAS

DINNER IDEAS

SHOPPING LIST	PRICE	NOTE

SUNDAY	Cal. (kcal)	Net Carb (g)	Fat (g)	Protein (g)	Sugar (g)
BREAKFAST					
LUNCH					
DINNER					
Total Daily Nutrition Fact					

85

MONDAY	Cal. (kcal)	Net Carb (g)	Fat (g)	Protein (g)	Sugar (g)
BREAKFAST					
LUNCH					
DINNER					
Total Daily Nutrition Fact					

TUESDAY	Cal. (kcal)	Net Carb (g)	Fat (g)	Protein (g)	Sugar (g)
BREAKFAST					
LUNCH					
DINNER					
Total Daily Nutrition Fact					

WEDNESDAY	Cal. (kcal)	Net Carb (g)	Fat (g)	Protein (g)	Sugar (g)
BREAKFAST					
LUNCH					
DINNER					
Total Daily Nutrition Fact					

THURSDAY	Cal. (kcal)	Net Carb (g)	Fat (g)	Protein (g)	Sugar (g)
BREAKFAST					
LUNCH					
DINNER					
Total Daily Nutrition Fact					

FRIDAY	Cal. (kcal)	Net Carb (g)	Fat (g)	Protein (g)	Sugar (g)
BREAKFAST					
LUNCH					
DINNER					
Total Daily Nutrition Fact					

SATURDAY	Cal. (kcal)	Net Carb (g)	Fat (g)	Protein (g)	Sugar (g)
BREAKFAST					
LUNCH					
DINNER					
Total Daily Nutrition Fact					
Total Weekly Nutrition					

BREAKFAST IDEAS

LUNCH IDEAS

DINNER IDEAS

SHOPPING LIST	PRICE	NOTE

SUNDAY	Cal. (kcal)	Net Carb (g)	Fat (g)	Protein (g)	Sugar (g)
BREAKFAST					
LUNCH					
DINNER					
Total Daily Nutrition Fact					

MONDAY		Cal. (kcal)	Net Carb (g)	Fat (g)	Protein (g)	Sugar (g)
BREAKFAST						
LUNCH						
DINNER						
	Total Daily Nutrition Fact					

TUESDAY		Cal. (kcal)	Net Carb (g)	Fat (g)	Protein (g)	Sugar (g)
BREAKFAST						
LUNCH						
DINNER						
	Total Daily Nutrition Fact					

WEDNESDAY		Cal. (kcal)	Net Carb (g)	Fat (g)	Protein (g)	Sugar (g)
BREAKFAST						
LUNCH						
DINNER						
	Total Daily Nutrition Fact					

THURSDAY		Cal. (kcal)	Net Carb (g)	Fat (g)	Protein (g)	Sugar (g)
BREAKFAST						
LUNCH						
DINNER						
	Total Daily Nutrition Fact					

FRIDAY		Cal. (kcal)	Net Carb (g)	Fat (g)	Protein (g)	Sugar (g)
BREAKFAST						
LUNCH						
DINNER						
	Total Daily Nutrition Fact					

SATURDAY		Cal. (kcal)	Net Carb (g)	Fat (g)	Protein (g)	Sugar (g)
BREAKFAST						
LUNCH						
DINNER						
	Total Daily Nutrition Fact					
	Total Weekly Nutrition					

BREAKFAST IDEAS

LUNCH IDEAS

DINNER IDEAS

SHOPPING LIST	PRICE	NOTE

SUNDAY	Cal. (kcal)	Net Carb (g)	Fat (g)	Protein (g)	Sugar (g)
BREAKFAST					
LUNCH					
DINNER					
Total Daily Nutrition Fact					

MONDAY	Cal. (kcal)	Net Carb (g)	Fat (g)	Protein (g)	Sugar (g)
BREAKFAST					
LUNCH					
DINNER					
Total Daily Nutrition Fact					

TUESDAY	Cal. (kcal)	Net Carb (g)	Fat (g)	Protein (g)	Sugar (g)
BREAKFAST					
LUNCH					
DINNER					
Total Daily Nutrition Fact					

WEDNESDAY	Cal. (kcal)	Net Carb (g)	Fat (g)	Protein (g)	Sugar (g)
BREAKFAST					
LUNCH					
DINNER					
Total Daily Nutrition Fact					

THURSDAY	Cal. (kcal)	Net Carb (g)	Fat (g)	Protein (g)	Sugar (g)
BREAKFAST					
LUNCH					
DINNER					
Total Daily Nutrition Fact					

FRIDAY	Cal. (kcal)	Net Carb (g)	Fat (g)	Protein (g)	Sugar (g)
BREAKFAST					
LUNCH					
DINNER					
Total Daily Nutrition Fact					

SATURDAY	Cal. (kcal)	Net Carb (g)	Fat (g)	Protein (g)	Sugar (g)
BREAKFAST					
LUNCH					
DINNER					
Total Daily Nutrition Fact					
Total Weekly Nutrition					

BREAKFAST IDEAS

LUNCH IDEAS

DINNER IDEAS

SHOPPING LIST	PRICE	NOTE

SUNDAY	Cal. (kcal)	Net Carb (g)	Fat (g)	Protein (g)	Sugar (g)
BREAKFAST					
LUNCH					
DINNER					
Total Daily Nutrition Fact					

MONDAY	Cal. (kcal)	Net Carb (g)	Fat (g)	Protein (g)	Sugar (g)
BREAKFAST					
LUNCH					
DINNER					
Total Daily Nutrition Fact					

TUESDAY	Cal. (kcal)	Net Carb (g)	Fat (g)	Protein (g)	Sugar (g)
BREAKFAST					
LUNCH					
DINNER					
Total Daily Nutrition Fact					

WEDNESDAY	Cal. (kcal)	Net Carb (g)	Fat (g)	Protein (g)	Sugar (g)
BREAKFAST					
LUNCH					
DINNER					
Total Daily Nutrition Fact					

THURSDAY	Cal. (kcal)	Net Carb (g)	Fat (g)	Protein (g)	Sugar (g)
BREAKFAST					
LUNCH					
DINNER					
Total Daily Nutrition Fact					

FRIDAY	Cal. (kcal)	Net Carb (g)	Fat (g)	Protein (g)	Sugar (g)
BREAKFAST					
LUNCH					
DINNER					
Total Daily Nutrition Fact					

SATURDAY	Cal. (kcal)	Net Carb (g)	Fat (g)	Protein (g)	Sugar (g)
BREAKFAST					
LUNCH					
DINNER					
Total Daily Nutrition Fact					
Total Weekly Nutrition					

BREAKFAST IDEAS

LUNCH IDEAS

DINNER IDEAS

SHOPPING LIST	PRICE	NOTE

SUNDAY	Cal. (kcal)	Net Carb (g)	Fat (g)	Protein (g)	Sugar (g)
BREAKFAST					
LUNCH					
DINNER					
Total Daily Nutrition Fact					

93

MONDAY	Cal. (kcal)	Net Carb (g)	Fat (g)	Protein (g)	Sugar (g)
BREAKFAST					
LUNCH					
DINNER					
Total Daily Nutrition Fact					

TUESDAY	Cal. (kcal)	Net Carb (g)	Fat (g)	Protein (g)	Sugar (g)
BREAKFAST					
LUNCH					
DINNER					
Total Daily Nutrition Fact					

WEDNESDAY	Cal. (kcal)	Net Carb (g)	Fat (g)	Protein (g)	Sugar (g)
BREAKFAST					
LUNCH					
DINNER					
Total Daily Nutrition Fact					

THURSDAY	Cal. (kcal)	Net Carb (g)	Fat (g)	Protein (g)	Sugar (g)
BREAKFAST					
LUNCH					
DINNER					
Total Daily Nutrition Fact					

FRIDAY	Cal. (kcal)	Net Carb (g)	Fat (g)	Protein (g)	Sugar (g)
BREAKFAST					
LUNCH					
DINNER					
Total Daily Nutrition Fact					

SATURDAY	Cal. (kcal)	Net Carb (g)	Fat (g)	Protein (g)	Sugar (g)
BREAKFAST					
LUNCH					
DINNER					
Total Daily Nutrition Fact					
Total Weekly Nutrition					

BREAKFAST IDEAS

LUNCH IDEAS

DINNER IDEAS

SHOPPING LIST	PRICE	NOTE

SUNDAY	Cal. (kcal)	Net Carb (g)	Fat (g)	Protein (g)	Sugar (g)
BREAKFAST					
LUNCH					
DINNER					
Total Daily Nutrition Fact					

MONDAY	Cal. (kcal)	Net Carb (g)	Fat (g)	Protein (g)	Sugar (g)
BREAKFAST					
LUNCH					
DINNER					
Total Daily Nutrition Fact					

TUESDAY	Cal. (kcal)	Net Carb (g)	Fat (g)	Protein (g)	Sugar (g)
BREAKFAST					
LUNCH					
DINNER					
Total Daily Nutrition Fact					

WEDNESDAY	Cal. (kcal)	Net Carb (g)	Fat (g)	Protein (g)	Sugar (g)
BREAKFAST					
LUNCH					
DINNER					
Total Daily Nutrition Fact					

THURSDAY	Cal. (kcal)	Net Carb (g)	Fat (g)	Protein (g)	Sugar (g)
BREAKFAST					
LUNCH					
DINNER					
Total Daily Nutrition Fact					

FRIDAY	Cal. (kcal)	Net Carb (g)	Fat (g)	Protein (g)	Sugar (g)
BREAKFAST					
LUNCH					
DINNER					
Total Daily Nutrition Fact					

SATURDAY	Cal. (kcal)	Net Carb (g)	Fat (g)	Protein (g)	Sugar (g)
BREAKFAST					
LUNCH					
DINNER					
Total Daily Nutrition Fact					
Total Weekly Nutrition					

BREAKFAST IDEAS

LUNCH IDEAS

DINNER IDEAS

SHOPPING LIST	PRICE	NOTE

SUNDAY	Cal. (kcal)	Net Carb (g)	Fat (g)	Protein (g)	Sugar (g)
BREAKFAST					
LUNCH					
DINNER					
Total Daily Nutrition Fact					

MONDAY	Cal. (kcal)	Net Carb (g)	Fat (g)	Protein (g)	Sugar (g)
BREAKFAST					
LUNCH					
DINNER					
Total Daily Nutrition Fact					

TUESDAY	Cal. (kcal)	Net Carb (g)	Fat (g)	Protein (g)	Sugar (g)
BREAKFAST					
LUNCH					
DINNER					
Total Daily Nutrition Fact					

WEDNESDAY	Cal. (kcal)	Net Carb (g)	Fat (g)	Protein (g)	Sugar (g)
BREAKFAST					
LUNCH					
DINNER					
Total Daily Nutrition Fact					

THURSDAY	Cal. (kcal)	Net Carb (g)	Fat (g)	Protein (g)	Sugar (g)
BREAKFAST					
LUNCH					
DINNER					
Total Daily Nutrition Fact					

FRIDAY	Cal. (kcal)	Net Carb (g)	Fat (g)	Protein (g)	Sugar (g)
BREAKFAST					
LUNCH					
DINNER					
Total Daily Nutrition Fact					

SATURDAY	Cal. (kcal)	Net Carb (g)	Fat (g)	Protein (g)	Sugar (g)
BREAKFAST					
LUNCH					
DINNER					
Total Daily Nutrition Fact					
Total Weekly Nutrition					

BREAKFAST IDEAS

LUNCH IDEAS

DINNER IDEAS

SHOPPING LIST	PRICE	NOTE

SUNDAY		Cal. (kcal)	Net Carb (g)	Fat (g)	Protein (g)	Sugar (g)
BREAKFAST						
LUNCH						
DINNER						
	Total Daily Nutrition Fact					

WEEK 1

MONDAY	Cal. (kcal)	Net Carb (g)	Fat (g)	Protein (g)	Sugar (g)
BREAKFAST					
LUNCH					
DINNER					
Total Daily Nutrition Fact					

TUESDAY	Cal. (kcal)	Net Carb (g)	Fat (g)	Protein (g)	Sugar (g)
BREAKFAST					
LUNCH					
DINNER					
Total Daily Nutrition Fact					

WEDNESDAY	Cal. (kcal)	Net Carb (g)	Fat (g)	Protein (g)	Sugar (g)
BREAKFAST					
LUNCH					
DINNER					
Total Daily Nutrition Fact					

THURSDAY	Cal. (kcal)	Net Carb (g)	Fat (g)	Protein (g)	Sugar (g)
BREAKFAST					
LUNCH					
DINNER					
Total Daily Nutrition Fact					

FRIDAY	Cal. (kcal)	Net Carb (g)	Fat (g)	Protein (g)	Sugar (g)
BREAKFAST					
LUNCH					
DINNFR					
Total Daily Nutrition Fact					

SATURDAY	Cal. (kcal)	Net Carb (g)	Fat (g)	Protein (g)	Sugar (g)
BREAKFAST					
LUNCH					
DINNER					
Total Daily Nutrition Fact					
Total Weekly Nutrition					

100

WEEK 51

BREAKFAST IDEAS

LUNCH IDEAS

DINNER IDEAS

SHOPPING LIST	PRICE	NOTE

SUNDAY	Cal. (kcal)	Net Carb (g)	Fat (g)	Protein (g)	Sugar (g)
BREAKFAST					
LUNCH					
DINNER					
Total Daily Nutrition Fact					

MONDAY	Cal. (kcal)	Net Carb (g)	Fat (g)	Protein (g)	Sugar (g)
BREAKFAST					
LUNCH					
DINNER					
Total Daily Nutrition Fact					

TUESDAY	Cal. (kcal)	Net Carb (g)	Fat (g)	Protein (g)	Sugar (g)
BREAKFAST					
LUNCH					
DINNER					
Total Daily Nutrition Fact					

WEDNESDAY	Cal. (kcal)	Net Carb (g)	Fat (g)	Protein (g)	Sugar (g)
BREAKFAST					
LUNCH					
DINNER					
Total Daily Nutrition Fact					

THURSDAY	Cal. (kcal)	Net Carb (g)	Fat (g)	Protein (g)	Sugar (g)
BREAKFAST					
LUNCH					
DINNER					
Total Daily Nutrition Fact					

FRIDAY	Cal. (kcal)	Net Carb (g)	Fat (g)	Protein (g)	Sugar (g)
BREAKFAST					
LUNCH					
DINNER					
Total Daily Nutrition Fact					

SATURDAY	Cal. (kcal)	Net Carb (g)	Fat (g)	Protein (g)	Sugar (g)
BREAKFAST					
LUNCI I					
DINNER					
Total Daily Nutrition Fact					
Total Weekly Nutrition					

BREAKFAST IDEAS

LUNCH IDEAS

DINNER IDEAS

SHOPPING LIST	PRICE	NOTE

SUNDAY	Cal. (kcal)	Net Carb (g)	Fat (g)	Protein (g)	Sugar (g)
BREAKFAST					
LUNCH					
DINNER					
Total Daily Nutrition Fact					

MONDAY	Cal. (kcal)	Net Carb (g)	Fat (g)	Protein (g)	Sugar (g)
BREAKFAST					
LUNCH					
DINNER					
Total Daily Nutrition Fact					

TUESDAY	Cal. (kcal)	Net Carb (g)	Fat (g)	Protein (g)	Sugar (g)
BREAKFAST					
LUNCH					
DINNER					
Total Daily Nutrition Fact					

WEDNESDAY	Cal. (kcal)	Net Carb (g)	Fat (g)	Protein (g)	Sugar (g)
BREAKFAST					
LUNCH					
DINNER					
Total Daily Nutrition Fact					

THURSDAY	Cal. (kcal)	Net Carb (g)	Fat (g)	Protein (g)	Sugar (g)
BREAKFAST					
LUNCH					
DINNER					
Total Daily Nutrition Fact					

FRIDAY	Cal. (kcal)	Net Carb (g)	Fat (g)	Protein (g)	Sugar (g)
BREAKFAST					
LUNCH					
DINNER					
Total Daily Nutrition Fact					

SATURDAY	Cal. (kcal)	Net Carb (g)	Fat (g)	Protein (g)	Sugar (g)
BREAKFAST					
LUNCH					
DINNER					
Total Daily Nutrition Fact					
Total Weekly Nutrition					

Made in the USA
Middletown, DE
07 December 2019